· LUNCH-HOUR ·
Patchwork

15 EASY-TO-START (AND FINISH!) PROJECTS

Martingale

Lunch-Hour Patchwork: 15 Easy-to-Start (and Finish!) Projects
© 2018 by Martingale & Company®

Martingale®
19021 120th Ave. NE, Ste. 102
Bothell, WA 98011-9511 USA
ShopMartingale.com

Printed in China
23 22 21 20 19 18   8 7 6 5 4 3 2 1

Library of Congress Cataloging-in-Publication Data
is available upon request.

ISBN: 978-1-60468-899-3

MISSION STATEMENT

We empower makers who use fabric and yarn to make life more enjoyable.

CREDITS

PUBLISHER AND
CHIEF VISIONARY OFFICER
Jennifer Erbe Keltner

CONTENT DIRECTOR
Karen Costello Soltys

MANAGING EDITOR
Tina Cook

ACQUISITIONS EDITOR
Karen M. Burns

TECHNICAL WRITER
Debra Finan

TECHNICAL EDITOR
Amelia Johanson

COPY EDITOR
Durby Peterson

DESIGN MANAGER
Adrienne Smitke

PRODUCTION MANAGER
Regina Girard

COVER AND
INTERIOR DESIGNER
Kathy Kotomaimoce

PHOTOGRAPHER
Brent Kane

ILLUSTRATOR
Sandy Huffaker

Contents

Introduction

While Wednesday may be just the midpoint of a typical workweek for most, at Martingale our hump days are synonymous with Handwork Happy Hour—a scheduled time to come together for a quick bite and then to stitch away the rest of the lunch hour. We share our latest techniques, chat about projects to come, and sometimes even brainstorm book ideas. There's no better way to drop a bit of creative camaraderie into the middle of the week.

Enjoy this collection of easy-to-start (and finish!) patchwork projects to make by hand or machine, with a focus on both simplicity and style. Depending on your skill level, some items, such as the Pieced Flag Bunting (page 51), can easily be made in an hour. Others, such as the Emblem Pillow Pair (page 59), may require a few lunch hours. But the goal isn't necessarily to start and finish fast as much as it is to break up your busy day with some well-deserved time to stitch a little something awesome.

Need a new wristlet for a night out with the girls? Make a Log Cabin Zippered Wristlet (page 55) over lunch. Having book club at your house? Why not piece together the Fence Posts Table Runner (page 39)? Your group will be talking about more than this month's read. Whether you're in a fast-paced office, a hectic school, a busy shop, or holding down the home front, you'll be astounded by how your creative productivity is suddenly soaring.

Country Home POT HOLDER

designed and made by **BETH BRADLEY**

Bring a homey touch to your kitchen decor with a sweet and scrap-friendly patchwork house pot holder. This project also makes a thoughtful—and quick—housewarming or wedding-shower gift.

FINISHED SIZE: 8½" × 9"

MATERIALS

Yardage is based on 42"-wide fabric. A fat quarter measures 18" × 21".

⅛ yard of red print for house
Scrap of white print, at least 2" × 2", for window
Scrap of yellow print, at least 3" × 4", for chimney
    and door
⅛ yard of light blue print for background
1 fat quarter of blue print for roof, binding, and loop
Scrap of green print, at least 2" × 8½", for grass
12" × 12" square of fabric for backing
12" × 12" square of batting
1½ yards of ½"-wide black cotton rickrack for edging

HOT STUFF

If the pot holder will get straight-from-the-oven use in the kitchen, use a layer of heat-resistant batting, such as Insul-Bright, which contains metalized polyester film that reflects radiant energy back to its source.

CUTTING

All measurements include ¼" seam allowances.

From the red print, cut:
1 rectangle, 1¾" × 6½"
1 rectangle, 1½" × 4"
1 rectangle, 1½" × 3"
2 rectangles, 1½" × 2"

From the white print, cut:
1 square, 2" × 2"

From the yellow print, cut:
1 rectangle, 2" × 3"
1 square, 1½" × 1½"

Continued on page 8

Continued from page 7

From the light blue print, cut:
2 rectangles, 1½" × 6¾"
1 rectangle, 1¼" × 8½"
2 squares, 2" × 2"
1 rectangle, 1½" × 4"
1 rectangle, 1½" × 2"

From the blue print, cut:
1 rectangle, 2" × 6½"
1 rectangle, 1½" × 5"
2"-wide strips *cut on the bias* to equal 40"
    when joined

From the green print, cut:
1 rectangle, 2" × 8½"

MAKING THE BLOCK

Press the seam allowances as indicated by the arrows.

1. Sew the red 1½" × 2" rectangles to the sides of the white square as shown. Sew the red 1½" × 4" rectangle to the bottom of the unit to make a window unit measuring 3" × 4", including seam allowances.

Make 1 unit,
3" × 4".

2. Sew the yellow 2" × 3" rectangle to the left side of the red 1½" × 3" rectangle. Sew the pieced unit to the window unit to make a door unit measuring 3" × 6½", including seam allowances.

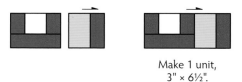

Make 1 unit,
3" × 6½".

3. Sew the red 1¾" × 6½" rectangle to the door unit to make a bottom section measuring 4¼" × 6½", including seam allowances.

Make 1 unit,
4¼" × 6½".

4. Cut a 7½"-long piece of rickrack. Place the rickrack along the top edge of the bottom section, aligning the upper curves of the rickrack with the raw edge as shown. Baste the rickrack in place.

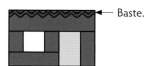

← Baste.

5. Draw a diagonal line from corner to corner on the wrong side of each light blue square. Place the squares on the blue 2" × 6½" rectangle as shown. Sew on the lines; trim the seam allowances to ¼". The roof unit should measure 2" × 6½".

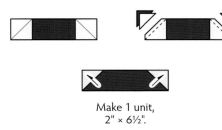

Make 1 unit,
2" × 6½".

6. Sew the light blue 1½" × 2" and 1½" × 4" rectangles to the yellow square to make a chimney unit measuring 1½" × 6½", including seam allowances.

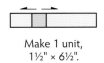

Make 1 unit,
1½" × 6½".

7. Sew the chimney unit to the roof unit to make the top section measuring 3" × 6½".

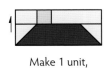

Make 1 unit,
3" × 6½".

8. Sew the top section to the bottom section to make a house unit measuring 6½" × 6¾", including seam allowances.

Make 1 unit,
6½" × 6¾".

9. Sew the light blue 1½" × 6¾" rectangles to the sides of the house unit. Sew the light blue 1¼" × 8½" rectangle to the top, and the green 2" × 8½" rectangle to the bottom. The block should measure 8½" × 9", including seam allowances.

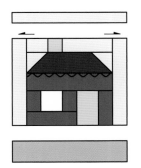 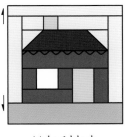

Make 1 block,
8½" × 9".

FINISHING THE POT HOLDER

For more details on quilting and finishing, go to ShopMartingale.com/HowtoQuilt.

1. Layer the quilt backing, batting, and block; baste the layers together. Hand or machine quilt as desired. The pot holder shown is quilted in the ditch around the house to add dimension and with an allover swirl design in the light blue background.

2. Using a thread spool or other small round object, trace a rounded line onto each corner of the pot holder; trim on the lines.

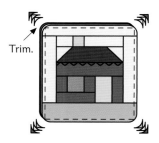

Trim.

3. Cut a piece of rickrack approximately 40" long. Place the rickrack around the edge of the pot holder, molding it around the corners and aligning the top curves of the rickrack with the raw edges. Overlap the ends of the rickrack, placing the tails off the edge of the pot holder. Baste the rickrack in place.

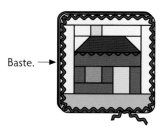

Baste. →

4. Fold the blue 1½" × 5" rectangle for the loop in half lengthwise; press. Unfold the rectangle, and then fold the raw edges to meet at the pressed crease. Refold the rectangle, enclosing the raw edges. Sew the long open edge.

Fold.

5. Join the ends of the blue bias strips with diagonal seams to make the binding. Press one long edge of the binding ¼" toward the wrong side. Starting in the middle of one side, sew the unpressed long edge of the binding to the edge of the pot holder with right sides together, gently easing the binding to round the corners.

6. Fold the binding toward the back of the pot holder, enclosing the raw edges. Fold the loop piece in half, and then place the ends under the binding fold on the back of the pot holder near the upper-left corner as shown. Slip-stitch the binding and loop in place.

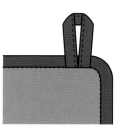

Patchwork TOTE BAG

designed and made by **JENNIFER MOORE**

Flying Geese and Square-in-a-Square blocks are among the most common patchwork shapes in quilting. Get your practice on by whipping up this handy, dandy tote. It's sized so that you can find whatever you need without having to go spelunking. Choose fabrics in bold contrast as shown, or pick your favorite hues.

FINISHED SIZE: 14" × 14"

MATERIALS

Yardage is based on 42"-wide fabric.

1¼ yards of white solid for bag front and back
1 square, 6½" × 6½", *each* of 6 different red and blue prints for Flying Geese and Square-in-a-Square blocks
¼ yard of red print for straps
½ yard of fabric for lining
2 squares, 17" × 17", of batting
2 strips, 3" × 30", of fusible interfacing

CUTTING

All measurements include ¼" seam allowances.

From the white solid, cut:
3 squares, 17" × 17"
16 squares, 3½" × 3½"
2 strips, 2" × 15½"
2 strips, 2" × 12½"

From the red and blue prints, cut:
2 squares, 6½" × 6½", each a different print
4 rectangles, 3½" × 6½", each a different print

From the red print for straps, cut:
2 strips, 3" × 30"

From the lining fabric, cut:
2 squares, 14½" × 14½"

MAKING THE BAG FRONT AND BACK

Press the seam allowances as indicated by the arrows.

1. Draw a diagonal line from corner to corner on the wrong side of each white 3½" square. Place a marked square on one end of a print rectangle, right sides together. Sew on the drawn line. Trim away the excess fabric, leaving a ¼" seam allowance. Stitch a

marked white square to the opposite end of the rectangle to make a flying-geese unit. Make four flying-geese units measuring 3½" × 6½".

Make 4 units,
3½" × 6½".

2. Place two marked white squares on opposite corners of a print square as shown. Sew on the drawn lines. Trim away the excess fabric, leaving a ¼" seam allowance. In the same manner, sew white squares to the remaining corners of the square to make a square-in-a-square unit. Make two units measuring 6½" × 6½", including seam allowances.

Make 2 units,
6½" × 6½".

3. Join the flying-geese units and square-in-a-square units in two vertical rows as shown. Sew the rows together. The block should measure 12½" square, including seam allowances.

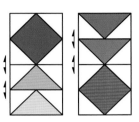 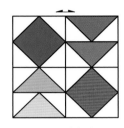

Make 1 block,
12½" × 12½".

4. Sew the white 2" × 12½" strips to the sides of the block. Sew the white 2" × 15½" strips to the top and bottom of the block. The bag front should measure 15½" square, including seam allowances.

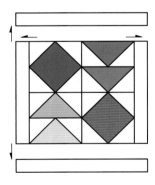

5. Layer a white 17" square, a batting square, and the bag front; baste. Quilt in the ditch along the seamlines.

6. For the bag back, layer a batting square between two white 17" squares; baste. Quilt a vertical line through the center of the layers. Quilt additional vertical lines 2" apart, working from the center quilted line outward, or quilt any desired design.

7. Trim the front and back pieces to 14½" square, keeping the front block centered.

8. Layer the quilted front and back squares right sides together. Stitch the sides and bottom, backstitching at the top edges. Clip the corners, and turn the bag right side out.

MAKING THE STRAPS

1. Fuse one interfacing strip to each red strip. Press each strip in half lengthwise. Open each strip and fold both long edges to the center crease; press.

2. Refold the strip in the center and stitch ⅛" from both long edges.

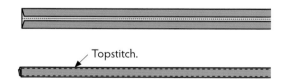

Topstitch.

FINISHING THE TOTE BAG

1. Measure 2½" to the left and right of the center of the bag front. Pin the ends of one strap to the bag front at the marks as shown, making sure the strap isn't twisted. Baste the straps to the bag front. Repeat for the bag back.

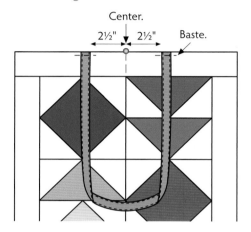

Center.
2½"   2½"   Baste.

2. Layer two lining squares right sides together. Stitch the sides and bottom of the squares, leaving a 4" opening in the bottom for turning. Do not turn right side out yet.

3. Tuck the bag into the lining; right sides together. Align the top raw edges and make sure the straps are between the lining and the bag pieces. Sew around the top edge.

4. Turn the bag right side out through the lining opening. Sew the opening closed by hand or machine.

5. Press the top edge of the bag; topstitch ¼" from the edge.

On-Point PICTURE FRAME

designed and made by **AMELIA JOHANSON**

Start with 3" squares in three coordinating fabrics to piece together the perfect border to fit across the top and bottom of an 8" × 10" photo mat. Combine with a bit of strip piecing to cover the sides of the mat, and you've created a pretty patchwork frame for a treasured photo.

FINISHED SIZE: 8" × 10"
FINISHED BLOCK: 1⅞" × 1⅞"
PICTURE FRAME OPENING: 4½" × 6½"

MATERIALS

⅛ yard *each* of coral dot, gray print, and blue print for piecing
⅛ yard of coordinating floral for binding
12" × 13" piece of thin cotton batting
8" × 10" piece of mat board with 5" × 7" opening
Glue stick
Spray adhesive
10" × 12" piece of butcher paper
4 self-adhesive photo corners (used in scrapbooking)
Water-soluble marker

CUTTING

All measurements include ¼" seam allowances unless otherwise stated.

From the coral dot, cut:
8 squares, 3" × 3"
1 strip, 1⅛" × 13½"

From the gray print, cut:
4 squares, 3" × 3"
1 strip, 1⅛" × 13½"

From the blue print, cut:
4 squares, 3" × 3"
1 strip, 1⅛" × 13½"

From the coordinating floral print, cut:
4 strips, 1½" × 10½"

NO TEMPLATE, NO PROBLEM

Trace around a 3" × 3" sticky note to cut perfect 3" squares. The note adheres to the fabric so it won't slip and is the ideal size for this project!

MAKING THE FABRIC FRAME

Press the seam allowances as indicated by the arrows.

1. Draw a diagonal line from corner to corner on the wrong side of each coral square. Place a marked square on a gray square, right sides together. Stitch ¼" to each side of the drawn line. Cut on the drawn line, press, and open to make a half-square triangle. Make eight units. Repeat using the blue squares and the remaining four coral squares.

Make 8 of each unit.

2. On all 16 half-square-triangle units, use a water-soluble marker to draw a line from corner to corner, perpendicular to the seam. Cut each on the drawn line. Rejoin the pieces as shown to make hourglass units. Make 16 hourglass units, eight of each colorway. Trim each unit to 2⅜" square.

2⅜" 2⅜"
2⅜" 2⅜"

Make 8 of each unit.

3. Sew a coral/gray unit to a coral/blue unit as shown. Make eight. Join four units to make the top of the frame and four units to make the bottom of the frame.

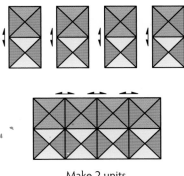

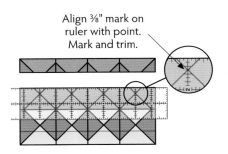

Make 2 units,
4¼" × 8".

4. With a rotary cutter and ruler, cut across the top and bottom frame pieces, ⅜" above and below the center row of on-point squares. Discard the cutaway fabric.

Align ⅜" mark on ruler with point. Mark and trim.

5. Sew the 13½"-long fabric strips lengthwise so that blue strip is centered between the coral and gray strips. Cut the pieced strip into two strips, 2⅜" × 6½", for the frame sides.

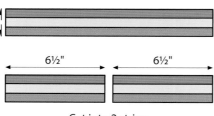

6½" 6½"

Cut into 2 strips.

6. Position one strip unit, right sides together, perpendicular to the bottom hourglass unit. Sew along the top edge using a ⅜" seam allowance and leaving the last ⅜" unstitched as shown. Repeat to sew the remaining strip unit to the other side of the bottom unit. Then join the top hourglass unit in the same manner.

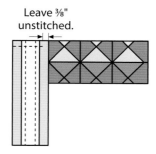

Leave ⅜" unstitched.

7. Trim the ⅜" seam allowance at the top and bottom edges of the frame to ¼". Attach 1½" × 10½"

binding strips to the sides of the frame. Repeat with the top and bottom binding strips as shown.

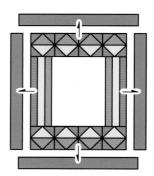

8. Place the patchwork frame over the piece of batting. With a water-soluble marker, mark the ⅜" seam allowance around the photo opening. Do not quilt in the marked seam allowance, which will be turned back onto the mat board and the batting from that area cut away. Quilt on the frame top and bottom in a mirrored zigzag (an X in each hourglass unit) to create an argyle effect, as shown in the photo on page 16.

PERFECT-COLOR QUILTING

If you want to quilt with a single thread over different color fabrics, try using a soft green rather than white or cream. It's not too dark against the lighter areas or too light against the darker-toned fabrics. Thanks, Karen Burns, for the tip!

9. Trim the batting away from behind the binding fabric, flush with the ¼" seam allowance. Trim the batting from the picture opening so that it is ⅜" inside the fabric edge. Fold back the gray strips of the frame sides at the corners of the photo opening to the point where they were left unstitched; clip vertically ⅜" into the top and bottom frame just across the seam allowance.

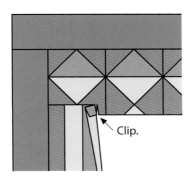

Clip.

APPLYING THE FABRIC FRAME TO THE MAT BOARD

1. Place the fabric frame right side down on an ironing board. Center the mat board (also right side down) over the frame. Apply glue from a glue stick on the wrong side of the mat board along the edge of the picture opening. Fold the fabric seam allowance (the section you clipped free in the previous step) back onto the glue. Turn the project over and make sure the on-point squares are positioned properly on the front. Turn the frame back over and press the seam allowance with the tip of the iron to the frame, setting the glue. Repeat for the upper edge and both side edges of the picture opening.

2. Folding the corners as you would when binding a quilt, fold the binding fabric edges around the ¼" seam allowance and onto the mat. Glue to secure as in the previous step. The binding edges should only show approximately ¼" around the frame on the right side.

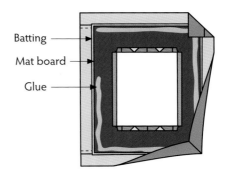

Batting

Mat board

Glue

3. On the butcher paper, trace around the outside of the frame and the inside of the picture opening. Cut out and trim to fit. Using a glue stick or spray adhesive, apply the paper backing to the frame to conceal the raw fabric edges. Apply self-adhesive corners to the chosen photo and adhere it to the paper backing centered in the picture opening.

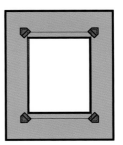

Sister's Choice TABLE TOPPER

designed and made by **BETH BRADLEY**

The octagon shape of this easy table topper lends a fun twist to the classic Sister's Choice block—a simple and versatile design that looks equally compelling in modern prints, bright solids, or reproduction fabrics. This speedy project requires only one big block, so you might be able to finish it in time to decorate your table tonight!

FINISHED SIZE: 16½" × 16½"

MATERIALS

Yardage is based on 42"-wide fabric. A fat quarter measures 18" × 21".

1 fat quarter of white solid for background
⅜ yard of navy dot for block and binding
⅛ yard *each* of navy floral and aqua print for block
¾ yard of fabric for backing
21" × 21" square of batting

CUTTING

All measurements include ¼" seam allowances.

From the white solid, cut:
4 squares, 3⅞" × 3⅞"
4 squares, 3½" × 3½"
1 square, 5" × 5"; cut into quarters diagonally to
    yield 4 triangles
4 strips, 1" × 12"
4 strips, 1" × 7"

From the navy dot, cut:
2 squares, 3⅞" × 3⅞"
2 squares, 3½" × 3½"
2 strips, 2½" × 42"

From the navy floral, cut:
2 squares, 3⅞" × 3⅞"
2 squares, 3½" × 3½"

From the aqua print, cut:
5 squares, 3½" × 3½"

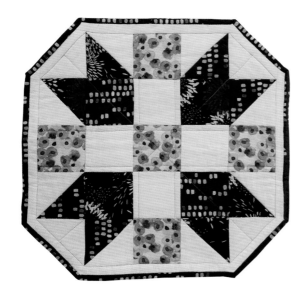

2. Lay out the half-square-triangle units; white, aqua, and navy 3½" squares, and white triangles in five rows as shown. Make sure to place the navy dot half-square-triangle units adjacent to the navy floral squares and vice versa. Join the units in each row; join the rows. The block should measure 15½" × 15½".

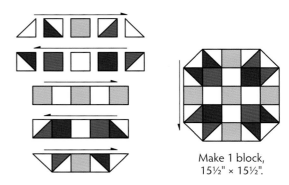

Make 1 block,
15½" × 15½".

MAKING THE BLOCK

Press the seam allowances as indicated by the arrows.

1. Draw a diagonal line from corner to corner on the wrong side of each white 3⅞" square. Place one marked square on a navy dot 3⅞" square, right sides together. Sew ¼" from both sides of the drawn line. Cut on the line to yield two half-square-triangle units. Make four white/navy dot half-square-triangle units measuring 3½" square, including seam allowances. In the same manner, make four white/navy floral half-square-triangle units.

3. With right sides together and raw edges even, position a white 1" × 7" strip across one corner of the block; stitch and press the seam allowances toward the strip. Repeat for the remaining three corners. Trim the ends of the strips even with the edges of the block.

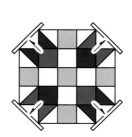 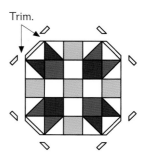

Trim.

Make 4 of each unit,
3½" × 3½".

Mitering octagonal corners requires folding the binding at an angle larger than the 90° corners of most quilts.

FINISHING THE TABLE TOPPER

For more details on quilting and finishing, go to ShopMartingale.com/HowtoQuilt.

1. Layer the backing, batting, and quilt top; baste the layers together. Hand or machine quilt. The table topper shown is quilted in the ditch to add dimension, and then across the block diagonally, horizontally, and vertically to emphasize the patchwork design.

2. Use the 2½"-wide navy dot strips to make double-fold binding. The angles of the octagon corners are larger than the 90° corners of most quilts, so mitering the corners requires folding the binding at a larger angle. Sew the binding along the edge of the quilt, ending ¼" before each corner; fold the binding back on itself, matching the angle of the adjacent table-topper edge. Fold the binding back toward the table topper, aligning the raw edges of the binding with the raw edges of the table topper, and then continue sewing the binding in place.

4. Using the same technique, sew one white 1" × 12" strip to each long side of the block; press away from the block. Trim the ends of the strips even with the block edges.

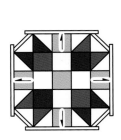
Trim.
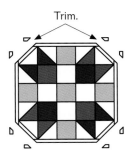

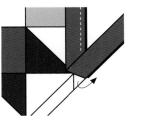
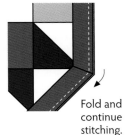
Fold and continue stitching.

3. Fold the binding to the back of the table topper and hand stitch the edges in place.

Zigzag Triangles PILLOW

designed and made by **JEMIMA FLENDT**

Equilateral triangles in two sizes come together to create zigs and zags and dramatic diamonds, all nestled together in this boldly pieced pillow top.

FINISHED SIZE: 20¾" × 20½"

MATERIALS

Yardage is based on 42"-wide fabric. A fat quarter measures 18" × 21". A fat eighth measures 9" × 21".

1 fat eighth of yellow print for triangles
1 fat quarter *each* of navy, aqua, and lime green
   prints for triangles
¾ yard of black-and-white print for side triangles
   and backing
¼ yard of navy fabric for binding
24" × 24" square of batting
20" × 20" pillow insert
Template plastic or 60° triangle ruler
Water-soluble marker

EASY EQUILATERAL TRIANGLES

The triangles for this project were cut using a 60° equilateral triangle ruler that has the "tip" cut off so that the triangles align neatly during sewing. If you don't have such a ruler, use the patterns on page 29 to make plastic templates.

CUTTING

All measurements include ¼" seam allowances.

From the yellow print, cut:
1 strip, 3" × 21"; cut into 8 small triangles

From the navy print, cut:
3 strips, 3" × 21"; cut into 24 small triangles

From the black-and-white print, cut:
1 strip, 5½" × 42"; cut into 8 large triangles
2 rectangles, 16" × 20¾"

From the aqua print, cut:
2 strips, 5½" × 21"; cut into 8 large triangles

Continued on page 26

Continued from page 25

From the lime green print, cut:

2 strips, 5½" × 21"; cut into 8 large triangles

From the binding fabric, cut:

2 strips, 2½" × 42"

MAKING THE PILLOW FRONT

Press the seam allowances as indicated by the arrows.

1. Place a yellow triangle and navy triangle right sides together, with a flat base of the yellow triangle and the blunt tip of the navy triangle along the bottom edge. Pin, and then sew along the right side.

2. Repeat step 1 with two navy triangles. Press the seam allowances toward the top navy triangle.

Make 4 of each unit.

3. Place the double-navy triangle unit right sides together with the yellow/navy triangle unit, aligning the top raw edges. One point of the yellow triangle will be facing upward, with a flat side along the bottom. Line up the tips of the triangles; pin in place and sew along the top raw edge. Press the seam allowances open. Make four sets.

Make 4 sets.

PRESS, DON'T IRON

The side edges of the triangles are cut on the bias, so be careful not to stretch and distort them while pressing.

4. Make a reverse yellow/navy unit following steps 1–3, mirroring the process to layer the triangles right sides together but sewing the *left* side. When the two triangle sets are joined, the yellow triangle will have a point facing downward and a flat side along the top. Make four sets.

Make 4 sets.

5. Make a row of zigzag triangles with two black-and-white triangles, two matching yellow/navy triangle sets, two aqua triangles, and two lime green triangles as shown. Pin the triangles in place and sew along the row, making sure to line up the triangles. Press. Trim off the remaining tips. Make two rows of this arrangement and two rows in a mirror image. Each row should be approximately 5½" tall.

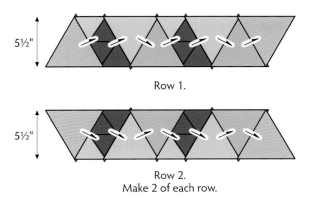

5½"

Row 1.

5½"

Row 2.
Make 2 of each row.

6. Alternate the rows and sew together as shown. Make sure to match up the points of the triangles from row to row, so that the points finish neatly. Press the seam allowances open. The rows should measure approximately 5" tall.

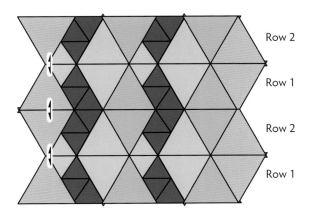

Row 2

Row 1

Row 2

Row 1

7. Using a rotary cutter and a long ruler, trim the ¼" seam allowance along the right and left sides of the black-and-white triangles, as shown. The lines should be ¼" to the right of the lime green row of triangles and ¼" to the left of the two yellow triangles.

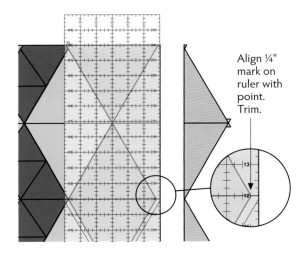

Align ¼" mark on ruler with point. Trim.

8. Lay the completed pillow front on top of the batting; baste using your preferred method. Quilt the pillow top. The featured pillow is machine quilted in lines following the zigzag pattern of the design and then again with horizontal lines on either side of the seamlines. Trim the excess batting from the pillow top. For more details on quilting, go to ShopMartingale.com/HowtoQuilt.

backing piece so that it overlaps the first backing. Pin through all layers and stitch around the pillow with ⅛" seam allowance.

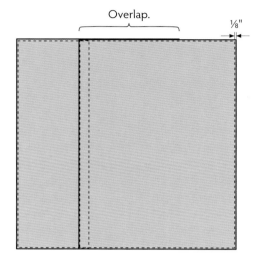

Overlap. ⅛"

FINISHING THE PILLOW

1. To make the envelope pillow back, apply a double hem along one long edge of each 16" × 20¾" rectangle. Fold under the raw edge ½", press, and then fold over another 1" and press again. Stitch the open side edges closed and stitch along the folded edge to give a neat finish.

2. Place the completed pillow front on a flat surface, right side down. Place one backing piece on top with the right side up, matching the raw edges at the top and sides. The hemmed edge should run along the front panel vertically. Place the second

3. Join the binding strips end to end and press the seam allowances in one direction. Press the entire strip in half lengthwise with wrong sides together.

4. Starting along one side of the pillow, not quite at the halfway point, sew the binding strip to the right side of the pillow top, mitering the corners as you go. Stop about 6" from where you started. Join the ends and cut off the excess. Continue sewing the binding to the pillow top. Fold over the binding and slip-stitch it into place along the back seamline.

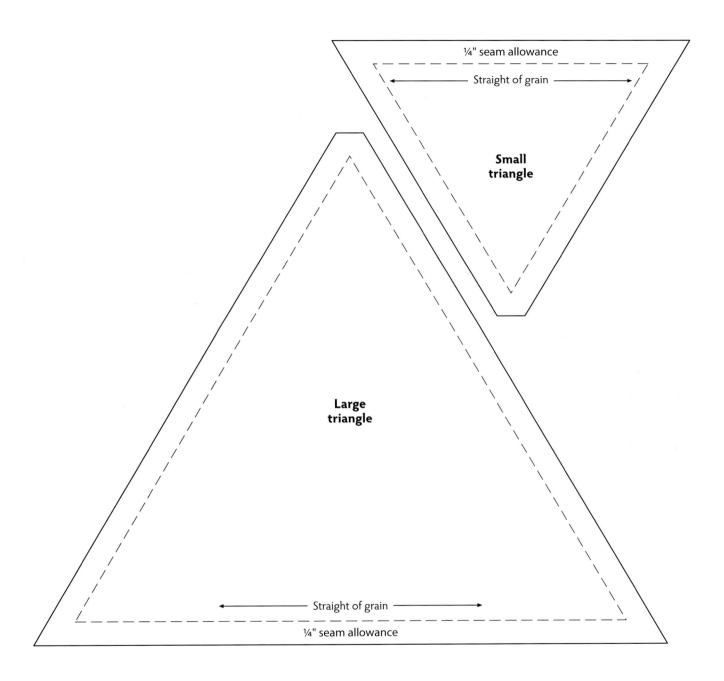

¼" seam allowance

Straight of grain

Small triangle

Large triangle

Straight of grain

¼" seam allowance

Bluebird WALL HANGING

designed and made by **SANDRA CLEMONS**

Bright and cheery, this paper-pieced Bluebird block takes flight on a quilted wall hanging. Imagine it, too, as a flock, each bird repeated in a different blue mini print on a larger quilt, throw, or runner. It's a perfect design for the bird lovers in your life, and it ushers in a sense of spring year-round.

FINISHED SIZE: 13½" × 13½"

MATERIALS

Yardage is based on 42"-wide fabric. A fat quarter measures 18" × 21".

1 fat quarter of white print for background
1 fat quarter of blue print for bird and outer border
Scrap of red print, at least 4" × 4", for breast
1 rectangle, 5" × 12", of green print for beak
    and inner border
¼ yard of navy solid for binding
15" × 15" square of fabric for backing
15" × 15" square of batting

CUTTING

Cutting instructions are for generously sized fabric pieces to allow flexibility for beginners. If you're experienced with foundation piecing, consider adjusting the size of the pieces to minimize waste. Label all pieces to keep them organized. All other measurements (for unlabeled pieces) include ¼" seam allowances.

From the white print, cut:
1 rectangle, 4" × 9" (F5)
2 rectangles, 5" × 7" (A1, D2)
3 squares, 4½" × 4½" (A3, B2, B3)
4 squares, 3½" × 3½" (C2, D3, F2, F3)
1 square, 2" × 2" (E3)

From the blue print, cut:
2 strips, 2½" × 13½"
2 strips, 2½" × 9½"
1 rectangle, 5" × 7" (C1)
1 rectangle, 2" × 6" (D1)
2 rectangles, 3" × 5" (B1, E1)
2 squares, 3½" × 3½" (A2, F4)

From the red print, cut:
1 square, 4" × 4" (F1)

Continued on page 32

Continued from page 31

From the green print, cut:
2 strips, 1" × 9½"
2 strips, 1" × 8½"
1 square, 2" x 2" (E2)

From the navy solid, cut:
2 strips, 2½" × 42"

PIECING THE FOUNDATION UNITS

For more details on paper foundation piecing, go to ShopMartingale.com/HowtoQuilt for free downloadable information.

1. Make 1 copy of each of foundation units A–F on pages 34–37.

2. Foundation piece the units as follows.

Unit A
Piece 1: white
Piece 2: blue
Piece 3: white

Unit B
Piece 1: blue
Piece 2: white
Piece 3: white

Unit C
Piece 1: blue
Piece 2: white

Unit D
Piece 1: blue
Piece 2: white
Piece 3: white

Unit E
Piece 1: blue
Piece 2: green
Piece 3: white

Unit F
Piece 1: red
Piece 2: white
Piece 3: white
Piece 4: blue
Piece 5: white

ASSEMBLING THE BLOCK

Press the seam allowances as indicated by the arrows.

1. Sew unit A to unit B.

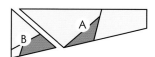

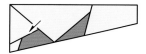

2. Sew unit C to unit D.

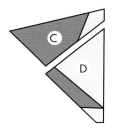
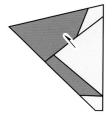

3. Sew unit E to unit F.

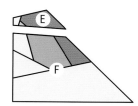
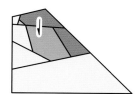

4. Sew unit C/D to unit E/F. Sew unit A/B to the top to complete the block. The block should measure 8½" square, including seam allowances.

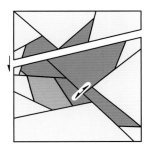

5. Sew the 1" × 8½" green strips to the sides of the block. Sew the 1" × 9½" green strips to the top and bottom of the block.

6. Sew the 2½" × 9½" blue strips to the sides of the quilt. Sew the 2½" × 13½" blue strips to the top and bottom of the wall hanging.

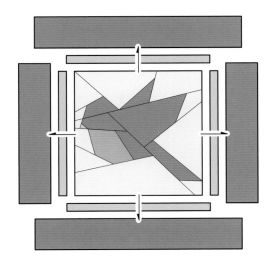

FINISHING THE WALL HANGING

For more details on these finishing steps, go to ShopMartingale.com/HowtoQuilt.

1. Layer the backing, batting, and quilt top; baste the layers together. Hand or machine quilt. The quilt shown is machine quilted with randomly spaced horizontal lines.

2. Add a hanging sleeve to the back of the wall hanging.

3. Use the navy 2½"-wide strips to make double-fold binding and attach it to the wall hanging.

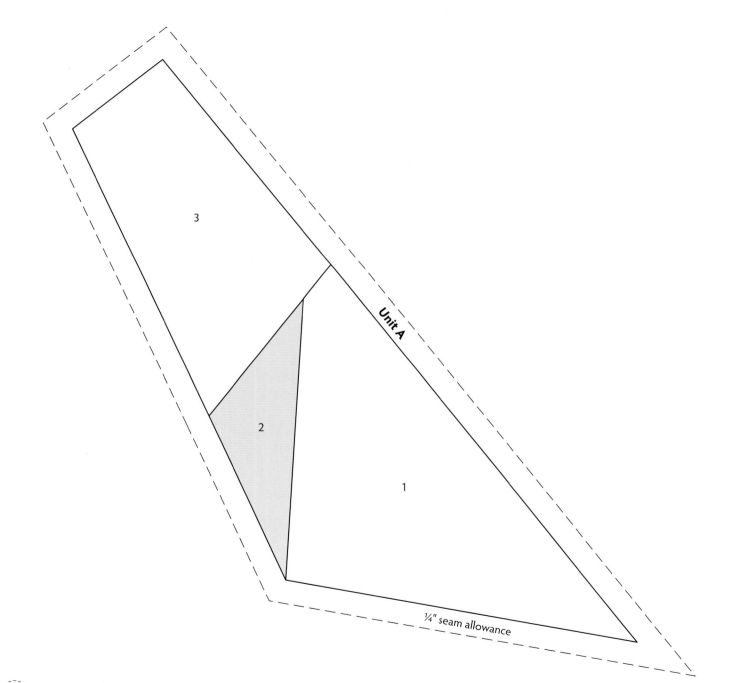

3

2

1

Unit A

¼" seam allowance

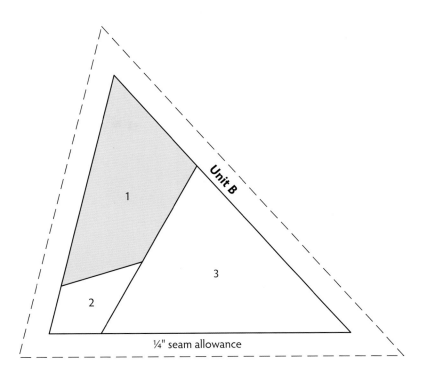

Unit B

1

2

3

¼" seam allowance

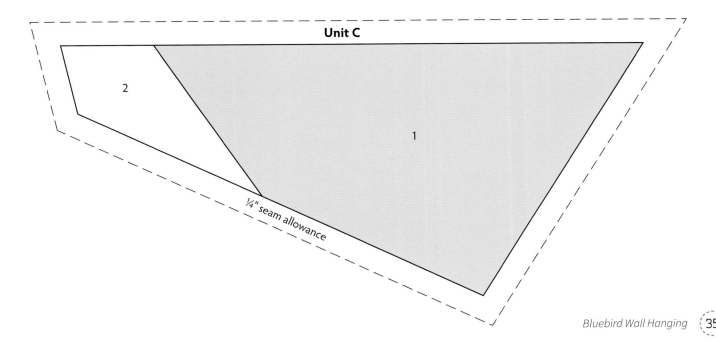

Unit C

2

1

¼" seam allowance

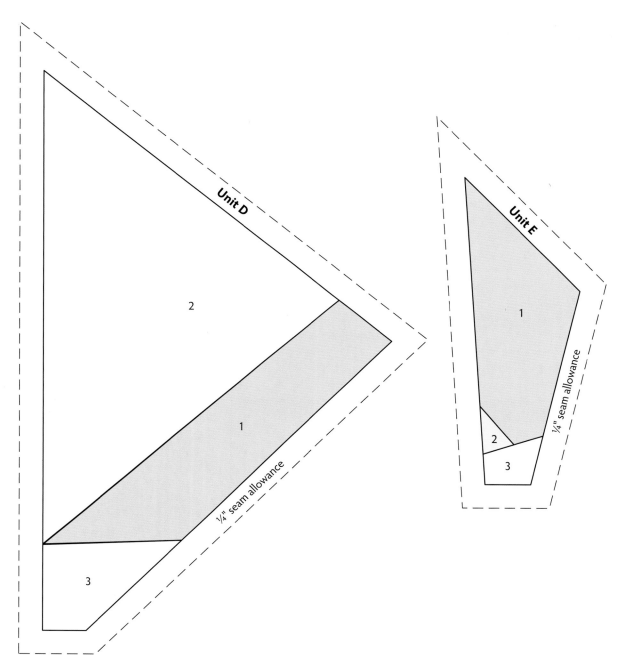

Unit D

2

1

3

¼" seam allowance

Unit E

1

2

3

¼" seam allowance

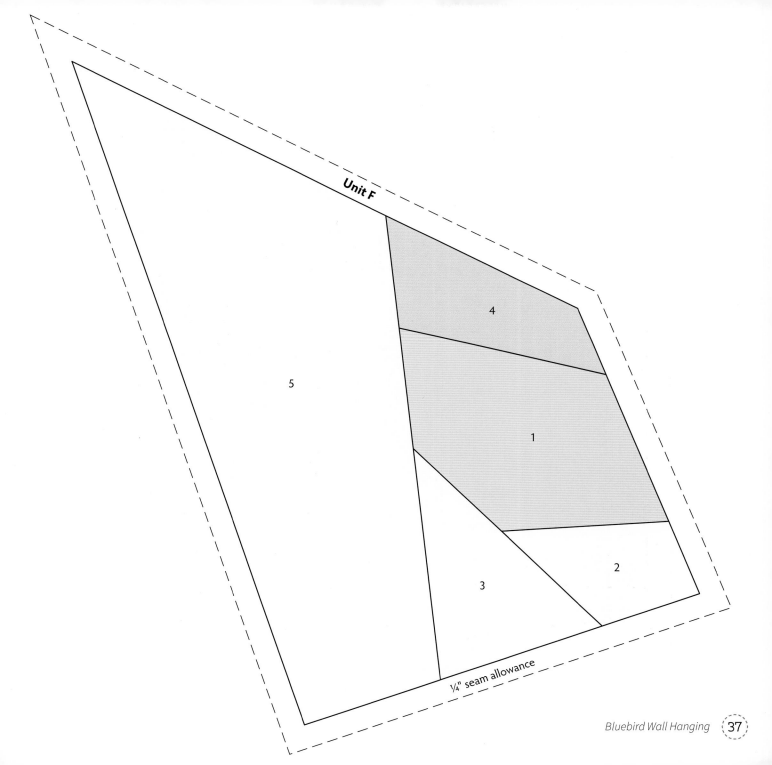

Unit F

5

4

1

3

2

¼" seam allowance

Fence Posts TABLE RUNNER

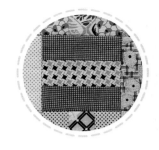

designed and made by **KAREN COSTELLO SOLTYS**

Whether you need a gift in a hurry or simply want to spruce up your decor at home, this table runner will fit the bill. Easy Rail Fence blocks team beautifully with a gray cotton-linen blend in a striking yet satisfyingly quick-to-piece runner.

FINISHED RUNNER: 18½" × 50½"
FINISHED RAIL FENCE BLOCK: 3" × 3"

MATERIALS

Yardage is based on 42"-wide fabric. A fat eighth measures 9" × 21".

12 fat eighths of assorted gray (low-volume) prints for blocks

12 fat eighths of assorted bright prints for blocks and binding

1 yard of gray woven cotton-linen blend for ends of runner and binding

1½ yards of fabric for backing*

22" × 55" piece of low-loft batting

*If you don't mind having a seam in the backing, ¾ yard will be sufficient.

CUTTING

All measurements include ¼" seam allowances.

From *each* gray print, cut:
1 strip, 1½" × 21"; trim the selvage and then cut each strip into 2 strips, 1½" × 10½"* (24 total)

From *each* bright print, cut:
1 strip, 1½" × 10½" (12 total)
1 strip, 2½" × 9" (12 total)

From the gray woven blend, cut:
1 strip, 18½" × 42"; crosscut into:
    1 piece, 12½" × 18½"
    1 piece, 18½" × 20½"
1 strip, 2½" × 42"

*If your strip doesn't measure at least 21" after removing selvages, you'll need to cut 2 strips.

MAKING THE RAIL FENCE BLOCKS

Press the seam allowances as indicated by the arrows.

1. Using two matching gray strips and one bright strip, make a strip set with the bright fabric in the middle. Make 12 strip sets measuring 3½" × 10½".

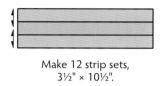

Make 12 strip sets,
3½" × 10½".

2. Cut each strip set into three segments, 3½" wide. Measure and cut carefully, as you will need almost the entire strip to cut three segments. If you can't get three segments from each, simply cut additional strips from your fabrics and make additional strip sets. You'll need 36 segments, 3½" square.

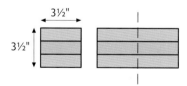

Cut 3 segments from each strip set.

ASSEMBLING THE RUNNER

1. Lay out the Rail Fence segments in six rows of six units each, rotating them so you alternate between vertical and horizontal seams. Rearrange until you're pleased with the color distribution.

2. Sew the segments together in rows and then sew the rows together. Press the seam allowances open or to one side. The completed patchwork block should measure 18½" square, including seam allowances.

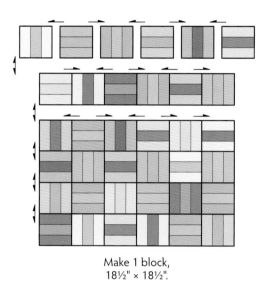

Make 1 block,
18½" × 18½".

3. Sew the gray rectangles to opposite sides of the patchwork block. Press the seam allowances toward the gray fabric.

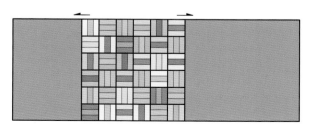

Runner assembly

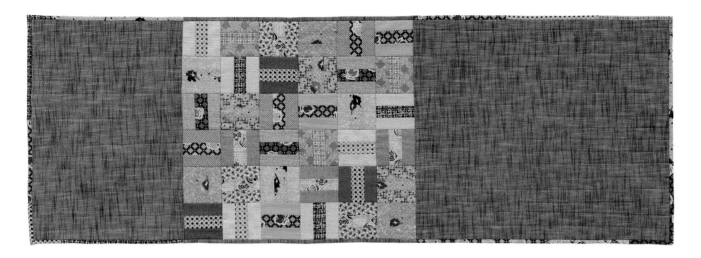

3. Trim the excess batting and backing, and then bind the runner using the 2½"-wide gray strip and bright strips. Karen used gray binding along the patchwork portion and bright binding along the gray sections.

OUT OF TIME?

If you're short on sewing time, pare the project down to just the patchwork section and turn it into an 18" square pillow. You'll spend less time doing the quilting and still have a lovely gift!

3. Trim the excess batting and backing, and then bind the runner using the 2½"-wide gray strip and bright strips. Karen used gray binding along the patchwork portion and bright binding along the gray sections.

FINISHING THE RUNNER

For more details on quilting and finishing, go to ShopMartingale.com/HowtoQuilt.

1. Layer the backing, batting, and patchwork top. Baste the layers together.

2. Hand or machine quilt. The featured runner is quilted using parallel straight lines spaced 1" apart, using the patchwork seamlines as guides.

Tiny Trees MINI-QUILT

designed and made by **CHRISTA WATSON**

Dress up your sewing space for the holidays with this adorable mini-quilt! It goes together so quickly, you may want to make another one and turn it into a festive companion throw pillow.

FINISHED QUILT: 18½" × 18½"
FINISHED BLOCK: 3" × 3"

MATERIALS

Yardage is based on 42"-wide fabric.

⅛ yard of brown print for tree trunks
⅝ yard of cream print for background*
¼ yard *total* of assorted green prints for trees
¼ yard of mint green print for binding
24" × 24" square of fabric for backing
22" × 22" square of batting

For best results, choose a nondirectional fabric for the background.

CUTTING

All measurements include ¼" seam allowances. Fabric pieces are cut generously for paper piecing. Label all pieces to keep them organized.

From the brown print, cut:
1 strip, 1½" × 42"; crosscut into 15 squares, 1½" × 1½" (piece 1)

From the cream print, cut:
1 strip, 3½" × 42"; crosscut into:
    2 rectangles, 3½" × 6½"
    2 rectangles, 3½" × 5"
    2 squares, 3½" × 3½"
    2 rectangles, 2" × 3½"
3 strips, 2¼" × 42"; crosscut into 30 rectangles, 2¼" × 4" (pieces 5 and 6)
4 strips, 2" × 42"; crosscut into:
    2 strips, 2" × 19"
    2 strips, 2" × 16"
    30 rectangles, 1½" × 2" (pieces 2 and 3)

From the assorted green prints, cut:
15 squares, 4" × 4" (piece 4)

From the mint green print, cut:
2 strips, 2½" × 42"

MAKING THE BLOCKS

For more details on paper foundation piecing, go to ShopMartingale.com/HowtoQuilt for free downloadable information.

1. Make 15 copies of the Tree block foundation on page 45.

2. Foundation piece in the following order, beginning with piece 1 and the brown print. Make 15 paper-pieced Tree blocks.

> **Piece 1:** brown print
> **Pieces 2 and 3:** cream print
> **Piece 4:** green print
> **Pieces 5 and 6:** cream print

COLOR CODING

When paper piecing, use colored pencils to color each piece of your template to correspond with the color fabric you will be using. This way, you don't need to keep checking which color fabric you will need for each numbered piece.

3. The blocks should measure 3½" square, including seam allowances.

Make 15 blocks,
3½" × 3½".

ASSEMBLING THE QUILT

1. Lay out the Tree blocks and cream background squares and rectangles in five rows as shown in the quilt assembly diagram below.

2. Sew the pieces into rows; join the rows. The quilt center should measure 15½" square, including seam allowances.

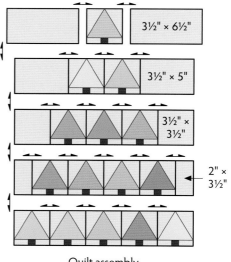

Quilt assembly

FINISHING THE QUILT

For more details on quilting and finishing, go to ShopMartingale.com/HowtoQuilt.

1. Layer the backing, batting, and quilt top; baste the layers together. Hand or machine quilt. The project shown is quilted with a continuous design of cursive capital *L*s in each of the trees and a simple stipple in the background.

2. Use the mint green 2½"-wide strips to make double-fold binding and attach it to the quilt.

3. Measure the length of the quilt center. Trim the cream 2" × 16" strips to this measurement. Sew the strips to the sides of the pieced quilt center.

4. Measure the width of the quilt, including the just-added borders. Trim the cream 2" × 19" strips to this measurement. Sew the strips to top and bottom of the quilt.

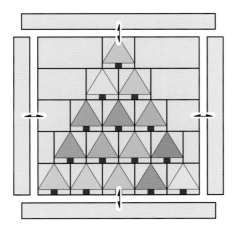

Adding borders

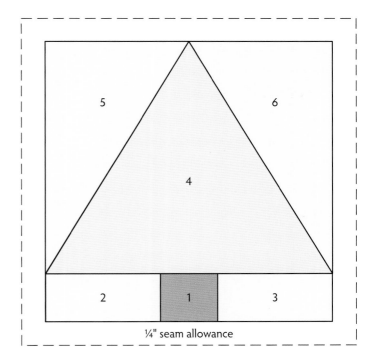

¼" seam allowance

Sweetheart NEEDLE BOOK

designed and made by **BETH BRADLEY**

Keep your hand-sewing needles and other tiny notions safe and sound in a cute-as-can-be patchwork needle book. The diminutive size makes it ideal for using up scraps, and this project is quick and easy enough that you can make one for all of your sewing friends.

FINISHED SIZE: 3¼" × 4" FOLDED

4" × 6½" OPEN

MATERIALS

Yardage is based on 42"-wide fabric.

10" square *each* of aqua floral, pink floral, and white dot for cover
6" square of pink wool felt for inner pages and pocket
5" × 8" piece of low-loft batting
1 child's hair elastic
⅜"-diameter button
Water-soluble marker

CUTTING

All measurements include ¼" seam allowances.

From the aqua floral, cut:
2 squares, 2" × 2"
4 squares, 1¼" × 1¼"
1 rectangle, 1" × 4½"

From the pink floral, cut:
1 rectangle, 3½" × 4½"
2 rectangles, 2" × 3"

From the white dot, cut:
1 rectangle, 4½" × 7"
2 rectangles, 1¼" × 3½"

From the pink wool felt, cut:
1 rectangle, 3½" × 6"
1 rectangle, 1½" × 2"

MAKING THE HEART BLOCK

Press the seam allowances as indicated by the arrows.

1. Draw a diagonal line from corner to corner on the wrong side of each aqua 2" square. Place a marked square on one pink 2" × 3" rectangle, orienting the line as shown. Sew on the drawn line. Trim away the excess fabric, leaving a ¼" seam allowance. The left unit should measure 2" × 3".

Make 1 unit,
2" × 3".

2. Repeat to make the right unit, orienting the marked line in the opposite direction as shown.

Make 1 unit,
2" × 3".

3. Draw a diagonal line from corner to corner on the wrong side of each aqua 1¼" square. Place a marked square on the upper-left corner of the left unit, right sides together, orienting the line as

shown. Sew on the drawn line. Trim away the excess fabric, leaving a ¼" seam allowance. Repeat to sew a marked square to the upper-right corner to complete the left unit. The unit should measure 2" × 3", including seam allowances. Complete the right unit in the same manner.

Make 1 of each unit,
2" × 3".

4. Join the left and right units, matching the seams at the center as shown. The Heart block should measure 3" × 3½", including seam allowances.

Make 1 block,
3" × 3½".

2. Using a thread spool or other small round object, trace a rounded line onto each corner of the front cover; trim on the lines.

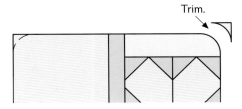

Trim.

5. Sew the white 1¼" × 3½" rectangles to the top and bottom of the Heart block to make a rectangle measuring 3½" × 4½", including seam allowances.

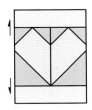

Make 1 block,
3½" × 4½".

ASSEMBLING THE NEEDLE BOOK

1. Sew the aqua 1" × 4½" rectangle between the pink 3½" × 4½" rectangle and the Heart block as shown. The cover should measure 4½" × 7".

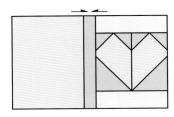

Make 1 cover,
4½" × 7".

3. Place the cover on the white 4½" × 7" rectangle, right sides together. Pinch the hair elastic to form a ½"-long loop; place the loop between the fabric layers at the center point of the inside-cover edge; pin. Center the layered pieces on top of the batting piece; pin. Sew around the perimeter of the cover through all layers, making sure to catch the elastic and leaving a 2" opening in the bottom for turning.

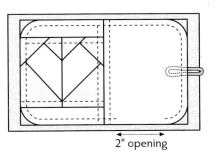

2" opening

4. Trim the seam allowances to ⅛", but don't trim the edges of the opening. Clip the corners. Gently turn the case right side out through the opening. Fold the opening edges toward the inside. Thoroughly press the case. Slip-stitch or whipstitch the opening closed.

5. Topstitch around the perimeter of the case. Hand or machine quilt. The needle case shown is echo quilted in the Heart block and channel quilted on the back rectangle.

FINISHING THE NEEDLE BOOK

1. If desired, embellish the felt 1½" × 2" pocket rectangle with a heart cut from a fabric scrap. The heart on needle case shown is stitched to the felt rectangle ¼" from the raw edge. Place the pocket on the felt 3½" × 6" rectangle, ½" from the lower edge and ¼" from the side edge as shown. Sew the sides and lower edge of the pocket.

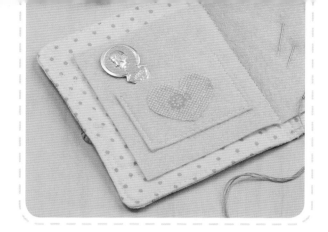

2. Center the felt rectangle, right side up, on the inside of the case; pin. Sew a vertical line through the center of the felt rectangle through all layers.

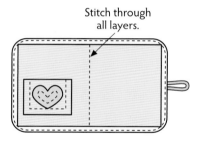

Stitch through all layers.

3. Fold the case in half, right side out; press. Fold the elastic to the front around the layers to determine button placement that will allow the case to close snugly; mark with a water-soluble marker. Hand stitch the button in place at the mark.

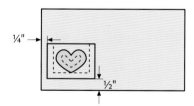

¼"

½"

Heart
Cut 1.

Pieced Flag BUNTING

designed and made by **JENNIFER MOORE**

Fabric buntings, aka garlands, have become a home decor staple. A whimsical way to add color and interest to any room, they've come a long way from party decor. Use this version, with its nautical sensibility, to dress up a nursery, patio, or powder room.

FINISHED FLAGS: 4" × 6"

MATERIALS

Yardage is based on 42"-wide fabric.

9 rectangles, 5" × 7", of assorted prints
¼ yard of white solid
50" length of 1"-wide woven ribbon or
    ½"-wide seam binding

CUTTING

All measurements include ¼" seam allowances.

From *each of 3* print rectangles, cut:
4 rectangles, 2¼" × 3¼" (12 total)

From *each of 6* print rectangles, cut:
2 rectangles, 2½" × 3½" (12 total)

From the white solid, cut:
6 rectangles, 4½" × 6½"
3 strips, 1" × 6½"
6 strips, 1" × 2¼"

MAKING THE BUNTING

Press the seam allowances as indicated by the arrows.

1. Sew two matching print 2¼" × 3¼" rectangles to opposite sides of a white 1" × 2¼" strip to make a pieced unit. Make two matching units measuring 2¼" × 6½", including seam allowances. Repeat to make three pairs of matching units.

Make 6 units,
2¼" × 6½".

2. Sew two matching units to a 1" × 6½" white strip to make a pieced flag. Make three pieced flags measuring 4½" × 6½", including seam allowances.

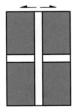

Make 3 flags,
4½" × 6½".

3. Sew two contrasting 2½" × 3½" rectangles together as shown. Make two matching two-patch units. Repeat to make three pairs of matching two-patch units.

Make 6 units,
3½" × 4½".

4. Sew the two-patch units together to make a pieced flag. Make three pieced flags measuring 4½" × 6½", including seam allowances.

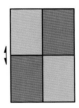

Make 3 flags,
4½" × 6½".

5. Layer a flag and white rectangle right sides together. Sew the sides and bottom, leaving the top open. Clip the corners and turn the flag right side out; press. Repeat for the remaining flags.

6. Fold the ribbon in half lengthwise; press. Position the flags inside the folded ribbon, allowing 2" to 3" between flags. Place the raw edge of each flag against the fold and pin each in place. Stitch the entire length of the ribbon, ⅛" from the edges, to secure the flags.

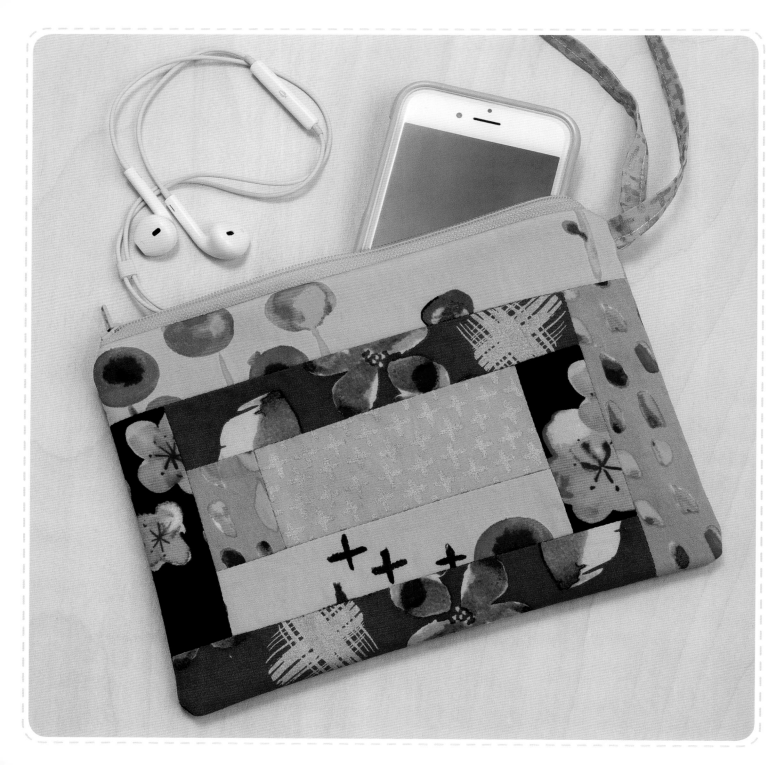

Log Cabin ZIPPERED WRISTLET

designed and made by **JENNIFER MOORE**

Bold fabrics in an easy-to-make wristlet blend a modern look to a traditional Log Cabin block. The patchwork is so simple, you'll be gifting these to all your friends—who, incidentally, will think you're a genius with needle and thread.

FINISHED SIZE: 8" × 5½"

MATERIALS

Yardage is based on 42"-wide fabric.

5 scraps of assorted prints, at least 3" × 9", for Log Cabin block
1½" × 14" strip of coordinating fabric for strap
2 rectangles, 6" × 8½", of fabric for lining
6" × 8½" piece of fabric for backing
2 rectangles, 6" × 8½", of fusible fleece
8" zipper*
Zipper foot for sewing machine

*If you can't find an 8" zipper, you can use a 9" or 12" nylon-coil zipper and trim it to fit.

CUTTING

All measurements include ¼" seam allowances.

From the 1st print scrap, cut:
1 rectangle, 2" × 4½" (A)

From the 2nd print scrap, cut:
1 rectangle, 1½" × 2" (B)
1 rectangle, 1½" × 5" (H)

From the 3rd print scrap, cut:
1 rectangle, 1½" × 5½" (C)
1 rectangle, 1½" × 8½" (I)

From the 4th print scrap, cut:
1 rectangle, 1½" × 3" (D)
1 rectangle, 1½" × 4" (F)

From the 5th print scrap, cut:
1 rectangle, 1½" × 6½" (E)
1 rectangle, 1½" × 7½" (G)

MAKING THE LOG CABIN BLOCK

Press the seam allowances as indicated by the arrows.

1. Sew rectangle B to the left side of rectangle A.

2. Add the remaining rectangles in alphabetical order, working counterclockwise around the center. The block should measure 6" × 8½", including seam allowances. Press the seam allowances away from the center block.

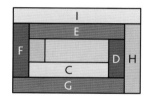

Make 1 block,
6" × 8½".

ASSEMBLING THE WRISTLET

1. Press fusible fleece onto the wrong side of the block, following the manufacturer's instructions. Repeat for the backing rectangle.

2. Fold the coordinating 1½" × 14" strap fabric in half lengthwise; press. Unfold the strip, and then fold the raw edges to meet at the pressed crease. Refold the strip, enclosing the raw edges. Sew the long open edge.

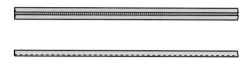

3. Pin the zipper, right side down, on the right side of the wristlet front, aligning the edge of the zipper tape with the raw edge of the top of the Log Cabin block. Using a basting stitch and a zipper foot on your sewing machine, baste the zipper to the wristlet front using a ¼" seam allowance.

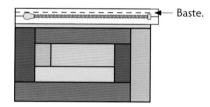

Baste.

4. Pin one lining rectangle to the wristlet front, aligning the top edges and enclosing the zipper. Stitch through all layers, using a zipper foot and a ¼" seam allowance.

5. In the same manner, pin and stitch the other side of the zipper between the wristlet back and the other lining rectangle.

6. Press the seam allowances away from the zipper and topstitch the fabric along both sides of the zipper. Unzip the zipper.

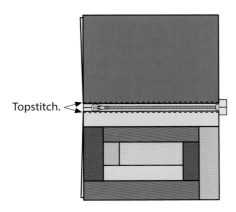

Topstitch.

7. Fold the strap in half to make a loop. Baste the ends of the loop to the right edge of the wristlet front, ½" below the zipper as shown.

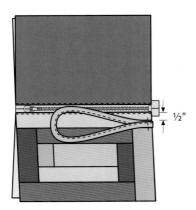

½"

8. Pin the front piece to the back piece, right sides together. Pin the lining pieces together with the zipper toward the lining pieces; the end of the zipper will be positioned so the zipper tape is right sides together. Take care not to stitch over the zipper pull or stop. Using a ¼" seam allowance, stitch around the edge, leaving a 3" opening in the bottom of the lining. Clip across all four corners.

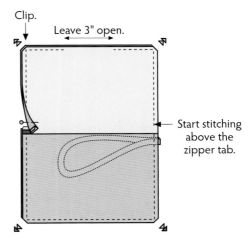

Clip.

Leave 3" open.

Start stitching above the zipper tab.

9. Turn the wristlet right side out through the lining opening. Hand or machine stitch the opening closed.

Emblem PILLOW PAIR

designed and made by **BETH BRADLEY**

This fun-to-make pillow pair requires just a few simple patchwork elements to create two complex-looking Southwest-inspired designs. The Block A pillow is shown opposite and the Block B pillow is on page 63. Use bold solid colors for a clean, graphic look that complements many decorating styles.

FINISHED SIZE: 16" × 16"

MATERIALS

Yardage is based on 42"-wide fabric. Fat quarters measure 18" × 21". The amounts listed are for making both pillows.

2¼ yards of white solid for background and backing
1 fat quarter *each* of red, gray, and teal solids for blocks
2 squares of batting, 20" × 20"
2 pillow forms, 16" × 16"

CUTTING

All measurements include ¼" seam allowances.

From the white solid, cut:
4 rectangles, 16½" × 19"
2 squares, 20" × 20"
5 strips, 2½" × 42"; crosscut into:
    4 rectangles, 2½" × 6½"
    18 rectangles, 2½" × 4½"
    32 squares, 2½" × 2½"
12 squares, 2⅞" × 2⅞"

From the red solid, cut:
8 rectangles, 2½" × 4½"
8 squares, 2⅞" × 2⅞"
4 squares, 2½" × 2½"

From the gray solid, cut:
6 squares, 2⅞" × 2⅞"
4 rectangles, 2½" × 4½"
8 squares, 2½" × 2½"
1 square, 4½" × 4½"

From the teal solid, cut:
6 rectangles, 2½" × 4½"
2 squares, 2⅞" × 2⅞"
12 squares, 2½" × 2½"
1 square, 4½" × 4½"

MAKING THE PATCHWORK UNITS

Press the seam allowances as indicated by the arrows.

1. Draw a diagonal line from corner to corner on the wrong side of six white 2⅞" squares. Place a marked square on a red 2⅞" square, right sides together. Sew ¼" from both sides of the drawn line; cut on the line to yield two half-square-triangle units. Make a total of 12 red/white half-square-triangle units. The units should measure 2½" square, including seam allowances.

Make 12 units,
2½" × 2½".

2. Mark the remaining white 2⅞" squares, and in the same manner, make eight gray/white, four teal/white, and four gray/red half-square-triangle units using the 2⅞" squares.

Make 8 units,
2½" × 2½".

Make 4 units,
2½" × 2½".

Make 4 units,
2½" × 2½".

3. Draw a diagonal line from corner to corner on the wrong side of each red 2½" square. Place two marked squares on opposite corners of the teal 4½" square as shown. Sew on the drawn lines. Trim away the excess fabric, leaving a ¼" seam allowance. In the same manner, sew red squares to the remaining corners of the teal square to make a center unit measuring 4½" square, including seam allowances.

Make 1 unit,
4½" × 4½".

4. Repeat with the gray 4½" square and four teal 2½" squares to make one gray/teal center unit.

Make 1 unit,
4½" × 4½".

5. Draw a diagonal line from corner to corner on the wrong side of 28 white 2½" squares. Place a marked square on one end of a red 2½" × 4½" rectangle, right sides together. Sew on the drawn line. Trim away the excess fabric, leaving a ¼" seam allowance. Stitch a marked white square to the opposite end of the rectangle to make a flying-geese unit. Make eight red/white flying-geese units measuring 2½" × 4½".

Make 8 units,
2½" × 4½".

6. In the same manner, make two teal/white, two white/teal, four gray/white, and four white/gray flying-geese units as shown using the 2½" × 4½" rectangles and 2½" squares.

Make 2 units,
2½" × 4½".

Make 4 units,
2½" × 4½".

Make 4 units,
2½" × 4½".

Make 2 units,
2½" × 4½".

MAKING BLOCK A

1. Sew one gray/white flying-geese unit to one white/gray flying-geese unit to make a chevron unit. Make four chevron units measuring 4½" square, including seam allowances.

Make 4 units,
4½" × 4½".

2. Lay out three red/white half-square-triangle units and one teal 2½" square in two rows of two as shown. Join the units in each row; join the rows to make a corner unit measuring 4½" square, including seam allowances. Make four corner units.

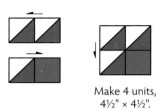

Make 4 units,
4½" × 4½".

3. Lay out two corner units, two white 2½" × 4½" rectangles, and one chevron as shown. Join the units to make a row. Make two rows measuring 4½" × 16½", including seam allowances.

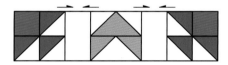

Make 2 rows, 4½" × 16½".

4. Sew a white 2½" × 6½" rectangle to each end of a red/white flying-geese unit as shown to make two rows measuring 2½" × 16½", including seam allowances.

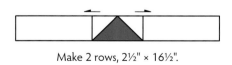

Make 2 rows, 2½" × 16½".

5. Lay out the teal/red center unit, two red/white flying-geese units, and two chevrons as shown. Join the units to make a row measuring 4½" × 16½", including seam allowances.

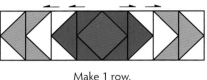

Make 1 row,
4½" × 16½".

6. Lay out the pieced rows as shown. Join the rows to make block A. The block should measure 16½" square, including seam allowances.

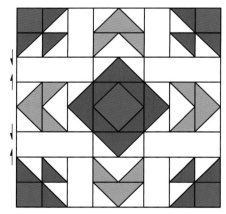

Block A.
Make 1 block, 16½" × 16½".

MAKING BLOCK B

1. Lay out one white 2½" square, two gray/white half-square-triangle units, and one gray/red half-square-triangle unit in two rows of two as shown. Join the units in each row; join the rows. Make four corner units measuring 4½" square, including seam allowances.

Make 4 units,
4½" × 4½".

2. Join a red/white and a teal/white flying-geese unit as shown. Make two red/teal flying-geese squares. In the same manner, join a white/teal and a red/white flying-geese unit. Make two red/white flying-geese squares measuring 4½" square, including seam allowances.

Make 2 units, 4½" × 4½". Make 2 units, 4½" × 4½".

3. Lay out two corner units, two white 2½" × 4½" rectangles, and one red/teal flying-geese square as shown. Join the units to make a row. Make two rows measuring 4½" × 16½", including seam allowances.

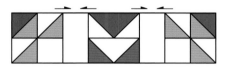

Make 2 rows, 4½" × 16½".

4. Lay out two white 2½" × 4½" rectangles, two teal/white half-square-triangle units, and one teal 2½" × 4½" rectangle as shown. Join the units to make a row. Make two rows measuring 2½" × 16½", including seam allowances.

Make 2 rows, 2½" × 16½".

5. Lay out the gray/teal center unit, two teal 2½" × 4½" rectangles, and two red/white flying-geese squares as shown. Join the units to make a row measuring 4½" × 16½", including seam allowances.

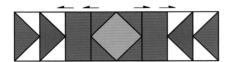

Make 1 row, 4½" × 16½".

6. Lay out the pieced rows as shown. Join the rows to make block B. The block should measure 16½" square, including seam allowances.

Block B.
Make 1 block, 16½" × 16½".

FINISHING THE PILLOWS

For more details on quilting and finishing, go to ShopMartingale.com/HowtoQuilt.

1. Layer a white 20" backing square, a batting square, and block A; baste the layers together. Hand or machine quilt as desired. The blocks shown were quilted with vertical lines spaced 1" apart. Repeat to quilt block B. Trim the backing and batting even with the edges of the blocks.

2. Fold a white 16½" × 19" rectangle in half to make a rectangle measuring 9½" × 16½"; press. Repeat for the remaining white rectangles. Sew ½" from each folded edge. Overlap the folded edges of two rectangles to create a 16½" backing square; baste the overlapped sections together in the seam allowances. Layer one quilted block on a backing square, right sides together. Sew around the perimeter. Clip the corners; turn the pillow cover right side out. Repeat to assemble the remaining pillow cover. Insert the pillow forms through the back openings.

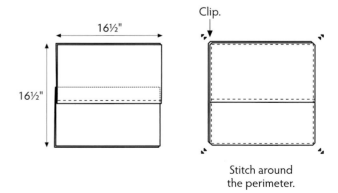

Stitch around
the perimeter.

Star Block TOTE

designed and made by **MELISSA MORTENSON**

Fussy cut a cool fabric motif for the center of the quilt block on this bold, striped tote. The bag is sturdy and roomy, making it just right to tote around town with you all day!

FINISHED BAG: 15" × 18"
FINISHED BLOCK: 12" × 12"

MATERIALS

Yardage is based on 42"-wide fabric. A fat quarter measures 18" × 21".

2 squares, 5½" × 5½", of pink gingham for block
1 square, 5½" × 5½", of pink print for block
1 fat quarter of white solid for block background and lining
1 square, 4½" × 4½", of fabric with fussy-cut design for block center
½ yard of fabric for bag lining
½ yard of navy-and-white stripe for bag
⅜ yard of 20"-wide Shape-Flex interfacing
⅞ yard of 40"-wide heavyweight fusible interfacing, such as Décor-Bond
½ yard of 40"-wide fusible fleece
1⅝ yards of 2"-wide cotton webbing for handles
Fray Check (optional)
Walking foot for sewing machine (optional)

CUTTING

All measurements include ¼" seam allowances.

From the white solid, cut:
1 square, 12½" × 12½"
4 squares, 4½" × 4½"
1 square, 5½" × 5½"

From the lining fabric, cut:
2 rectangles, 16" × 19"

From the navy-and-white stripe, cut:
2 rectangles, 16" × 19"

From the interfacing, cut:
1 square, 12½" × 12½"

From the heavyweight interfacing, cut:
2 rectangles, 16" × 19"
1 square, 12½" × 12½"

From the fusible fleece, cut:
2 rectangles, 16" × 19"

From the cotton webbing, cut:
2 pieces, 28" long

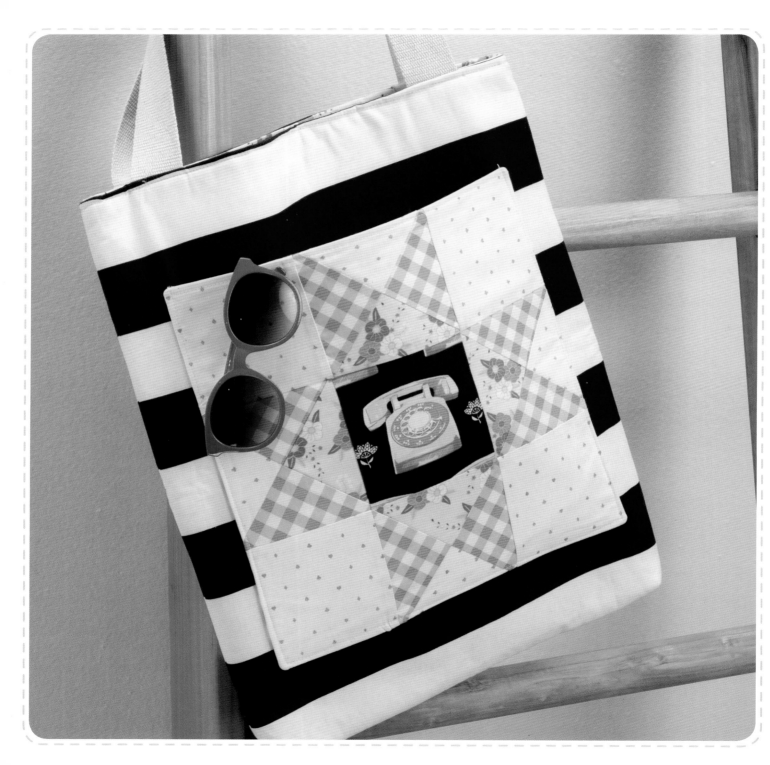

MAKING THE STAR BLOCK POCKET

Press the seam allowances as indicated by the arrows.

1. Draw a diagonal line from corner to corner on the wrong side of each pink gingham square. Place one marked square on the pink print square, right sides together. Sew ¼" from both sides of the drawn line; cut on the line to yield two half-square-triangle units. Repeat, using the remaining pink gingham square and the white 5½" square to make a total of four units.

Make 2 of each unit.

2. Place one print half-square-triangle unit on one white half-square-triangle unit, right sides together, with the gingham on opposite sides. Draw a diagonal line from corner to corner, perpendicular to the seam. Sew ¼" from both sides of the drawn line; cut on the line to yield two hourglass units. Repeat to make a total of four hourglass units, using the remaining half-square-triangle units. Trim the hourglass units to 4½" square.

4½"

4½"

Make 4 units.

3. Lay out the hourglass units, fussy-cut square, and white 4½" squares in three rows of three. Sew the pieces into rows. The block should measure 12½" square.

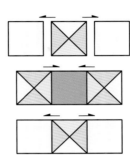 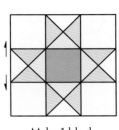

Make 1 block, 12½" × 12½".

4. Press the interfacing onto the wrong side of the Star block.

5. Press the heavyweight fusible interfacing onto the wrong side of the white 12½" square.

6. Layer the quilt block and fused square, right sides together. Stitch around the edges, leaving a 4" opening in the bottom for turning. Clip the corners, and turn right side out through the opening to make the quilt block pocket.

7. Press the pocket, turning the opening seam allowances inward so that they are flush with the sewn edges of the block. Stitch the top of the quilt-block pocket, ⅛" from the edge.

FINISHING THE TOTE BAG

1. Press the heavyweight interfacing onto the wrong side of the lining rectangles. Press the fusible fleece onto the wrong side of the striped rectangles.

2. Pin the pocket to a striped rectangle, centering it 3½" from the top raw edge of the rectangle. Stitch the sides and bottom of the pocket ⅛" from the edges, backstitching the top edges of the pocket to secure.

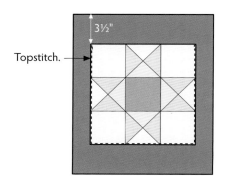

3. Cut a 1" square from the bottom corners of each bag rectangle and lining rectangle as shown.

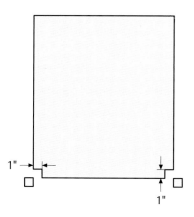

4. Apply Fray Check to each end of the webbing pieces. Allow to dry; then pin one strap to the bag front so that the outer edges of the strap are 2½" from the side of the bag. Baste in place, about ¼" from the top raw edge of the bag. Repeat with the remaining strap and bag back.

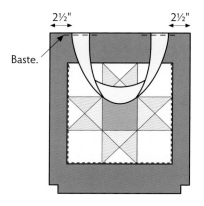

FUSSY CUTTING

There are plenty of tools and templates that enable you to frame the part of a motif you'd like to cut out, but in a pinch, simply tape around the chosen design with painter's or masking tape to envision what the finished fussy-cut piece will look like.

5. Pin the bag front and back pieces together, right sides together. Stitch together along the bottom and side seams using a ½" seam allowance. Press the seam allowances open.

6. Pinch the bottom corners of the bag so that the raw edges of the cutout corners are aligned and the side and bottom seams are on top of each other. Stitch using a ½" seam allowance.

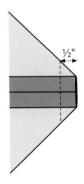

7. In the same manner, stitch the lining pieces together, leaving a 5" opening in the bottom seam for turning.

8. Slip the bag into the lining, right sides together. Pin the top edge, matching center fronts and side seams. If the lining and bag pieces do not align properly, adjust the lining side seams until the two pieces fit together correctly.

9. Stitch the bag to the lining ½" from the top raw edge. It's helpful, but not necessary, to use a walking foot for this step.

10. Turn the bag right side out through the lining opening, and press. Stitch around the top of the bag, ¼" from the edge. Stitch the lining closed by hand or machine.

Seaside COASTERS

designed and made by **KATE COLLERAN**

Add function and a pop of color to your home with a set of quick and easy coasters! You can choose any color combination; the blue and green coasters shown would look great in a seaside cottage. There are two different designs, each with binding to add a finishing touch.

FINISHED COASTERS: APPROXIMATELY 4⅝" × 4⅝"
FINISHED BLOCK: APPROXIMATELY 4⅛" × 4⅛"

MATERIALS

Yardage is based on 42"-wide fabric. The amounts listed are for making 4 coasters.

1 rectangle, 2" × 4", *each* of 4 assorted blue prints for four-patch units

2 rectangles, 3" × 6", of green print for blocks

1 square, 5" × 5", *each* of 2 contrasting blue prints for half-square-triangle units

2 rectangles, 3" × 6", of light blue print for blocks

¼ yard of navy print for binding

4 squares, 5½" × 5½", of blue print for backing

4 squares, 5" × 5", of batting

CUTTING

All measurements include ¼" seam allowances. The cutting instructions are for making 2 coasters of each design.

From *each* of the 4 blue print rectangles, cut:
2 squares, 1¾" × 1¾" (8 total)

From the green print, cut:
4 squares, 2¾" × 2¾"; cut each square in half diagonally to yield 8 half-square triangles

From *each* of the 2 contrasting blue print squares, cut:
4 squares, 2⅛" × 2⅛" (8 total)

From the light blue print, cut:
4 squares, 2¾" × 2¾"; cut each square in half diagonally to yield 8 half-square triangles

From the navy print, cut:
2 strips, 1½" × 42", for single-fold binding

MAKING THE BLOCKS

Press the seam allowances as indicated by the arrows.

1. Lay out one each of the blue 1¾" squares in two rows as shown. Sew the squares in rows; join the rows to make a unit. Make two four-patch units measuring 3" square, including seam allowances.

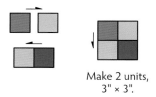

Make 2 units,
3" × 3".

2. Sew two green triangles to opposite sides of a four-square unit as shown. Sew a green triangle to each remaining side. Make two Four Patch blocks. Trim along all four sides, leaving a ¼" seam allowance.

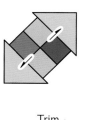

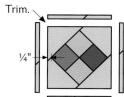

Trim.

¼"

3. Draw a diagonal line from corner to corner on the wrong side of the lighter of the blue 2⅛" squares. Layer two contrasting squares right sides together. Sew ¼" away from the drawn line on both sides. Cut on the line to yield two half-square-triangle units. Make eight half-square-triangle units measuring 1¾" square, including seam allowances.

Make 8 units,
1¾" × 1¾".

4. Lay out four half-square-triangle units in two rows; join the rows to make a pieced unit. Make two units measuring 3" square, including seam allowances.

Make 2 units,
3" × 3".

5. Sew light blue triangles to opposite corners of a pieced unit. Sew a light blue triangle to each remaining side. Make two Hourglass blocks. Trim the sides of each block, leaving a ¼" seam allowance. Don't worry about the exact size of the block. It should be about 4⅛" square, but having a ¼" seam allowance is more important than the size.

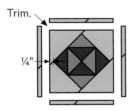

Trim.

¼"

FINISHING THE COASTERS

For more details on quilting and finishing, go to ShopMartingale.com/HowtoQuilt.

1. Layer each block with batting and backing; baste the layers and quilt. The Four Patch coasters are quilted with diagonal lines. The Hourglass coasters are quilted with a diagonal crosshatch.

2. Press a ¼" seam allowance on one long edge of each navy 1½"-wide binding strip toward the wrong side. Place one strip on the front of a coaster, right

sides together, aligning the edges. Stitch the first side, stopping ¼" from the corner, and backstitch 1 or 2 stitches.

3. Fold the binding up to make a diagonal fold. Keeping the fold in place, fold the binding straight down. The binding should be even with the edges of the coaster. Backstitching at the beginning and end, sew the next side, stopping ¼" from the corner.

  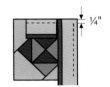

¼"

¼"

4. Continue folding and stitching the binding around the coaster, stopping ½" to 1" past the last corner. Remove the coaster from the machine and overlap the ends of the binding. Mark ½" from the point where the ends meet and trim the top piece of binding at that mark. Open the pressed edge, place the ends of the binding strip right sides together, and sew with a ¼" seam allowance. Finger press the seam allowances open. Finish sewing the binding to the coaster.

5. Fold the binding to the back of the coaster, covering the stitching line with the pressed edge of the binding. Hand stitch the binding in place, mitering the corners as you get to them.

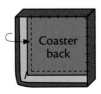

Coaster
back

Pretty Pinwheel CLUTCH

designed and made by **MELISSA MORTENSON**

Quilt blocks aren't just for quilts! Stitch a fun and colorful Pinwheel clutch to take with you on your next night out.

FINISHED CLUTCH: 10½" × 14"
FINISHED BLOCK: 3½" × 3½"

MATERIALS

Yardage is based on 42"-wide fabric

½ yard of white solid for background
1 square, at least 6" × 6", *each* of 6 assorted green prints
1 square, at least 6" × 6", *each* of 6 assorted pink prints
⅜ yard of fabric for lining
¾ yard 20"-wide fusible fleece
10" zipper*
Zipper foot for sewing machine

If you can't find a 10" zipper, you can use a longer nylon-coil zipper and trim it to fit.

CUTTING

All measurements include ¼" seam allowances.

From the white solid, cut:
4 strips, 3" × 42"; crosscut into 48 squares, 3" × 3"

From *each* green print, cut:
4 squares, 3" × 3" (24 total)

From *each* pink print, cut:
4 squares, 3" × 3" (24 total)

From the lining fabric, cut:
2 rectangles, 11" × 14½"

From the fusible fleece, cut:
2 rectangles, 11" × 14½"

MAKING THE BAG FRONT

Press the seam allowances as indicated by the arrows.

1. Draw a diagonal line from corner to corner on the wrong side of each white square. Place a marked square on a print square, right sides together. Sew ¼" from both sides of the drawn line; cut on the line to yield two half-square-triangle units. Trim the units to 2¼" square. Make a total of 96 half-square-triangle units.

Make 96 units.

2. Lay out four matching half-square-triangle units in two rows of two as shown. Sew the units into rows. Sew the rows together to make a Pinwheel block. Make a total of 24 Pinwheel blocks measuring 4" square, including seam allowances.

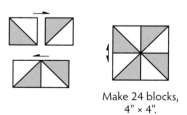

Make 24 blocks,
4" × 4".

3. Lay out the blocks into four rows of three, alternating green and pink prints as shown. Sew the blocks into rows. Sew the rows together. The bag front should measure 11" × 14½". Repeat to make the bag back.

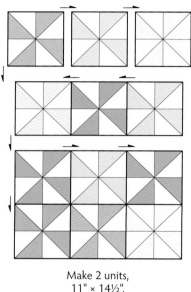

Make 2 units,
11" × 14½".

ASSEMBLING THE CLUTCH

1. Press the fusible fleece onto the wrong side of the clutch front and back pieces.

2. Pin the zipper, right side down, on the right side of the clutch front, aligning the zipper edge with the raw edge of one of the 11" sides of the clutch front. Using a basting stitch and a zipper foot on your sewing machine, baste the zipper to the clutch front using a ¼" seam allowance.

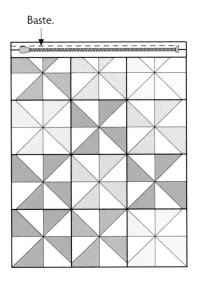

3. Pin a lining rectangle to the clutch front, aligning the top edges and enclosing the zipper. Stitch through all layers, using a zipper foot and a ¼" seam allowance.

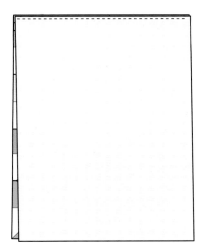

4. In the same manner, pin and stitch the other side of the zipper between the clutch back and lining pieces.

5. Press the seam allowances away from the zipper and topstitch the fabric along both sides of the zipper. Unzip the zipper.

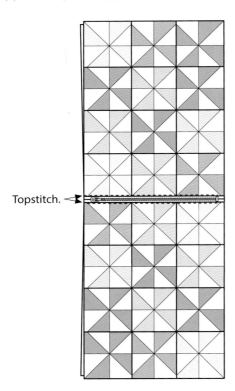

Topstitch.

6. Pin the clutch front to the back, right sides together. Pin the lining pieces together with the zipper toward the lining pieces; the end of the zipper will be positioned so the zipper tape is right sides together. Take care not to stitch over the zipper pull

or stop. Using a ¼" seam allowance, stitch around the edge, leaving a 3" opening in the bottom of the lining. Clip across all four corners.

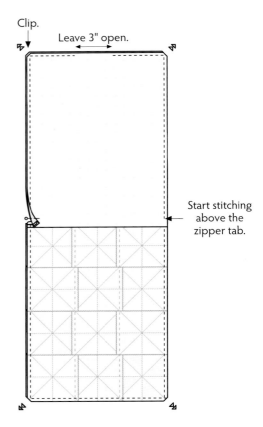

Clip.

Leave 3" open.

Start stitching above the zipper tab.

7. Turn the clutch right side out through the lining opening. Press the clutch. Hand or machine stitch the opening closed.

About the Contributors

Beth Bradley

Beth earned a degree in apparel design and feels very lucky to have turned her fabric obsession into her livelihood, as a clothing designer and sewing editor.

Sandra Clemons

The owner of Make It Blossom, Sandra designs fabric, quilts, and garments. She is an author and blogger who enjoys teaching quiltmaking and sharing her adventures as a wife and mother. Visit her online at SandraMakeItBlossom.com.

Kate Colleran

Kate is a quilt pattern designer and fabric enthusiast who thrives on encouraging creativity. She is known for her fun and fresh designs and for providing written instructions that are clear enough for beginners. Visit Kate online at SeamsLikeaDream.com.

Jemima Flendt

Jemima has always had a love for fabric, textiles, buttons, ribbons, and embellishments. With a background as a home economics teacher, she teaches quiltmaking classes and workshops. Jemima has been crafting and sewing since she was a child, and she enjoys inspiring others to be creative. She lives in Perth, Australia. Visit her at TiedWithaRibbon.com.

Amelia Johanson

Amelia is a University of Missouri graduate with degrees in journalism and home economics. She has been blessed to combine her passions for both the written word and fabric in her roles as a newspaper fashion writer, a sewing-magazine editor, and currently as an acquisitions and development editor at Martingale. Sewing is her go-to stress reliever.

Jennifer Moore

Jennifer and her husband, David Miguelucci, own and operate Monaluna, an organic fabric company based in Walnut Creek, California. Jennifer is a designer and textile artist who started the company in 2010 with a commitment to providing environmentally friendly fabrics for sewists and quilters. Visit Monaluna.com.

Melissa Mortenson

Melissa is an author and fabric designer and the founder of the blog Polka Dot Chair. She enjoys encouraging mothers and families to find simple inspiring DIY ideas for the home, plus sewing projects, holidays crafts, and tasty recipes. Visit Melissa at PolkaDotChair.com.

Karen Costello Soltys

Karen is a knitting, rughooking, quilting, movie-watching, reading, backyard chicken-raising enthusiast. When not pursuing those interests, she works at Martingale as its content director. Karen is the author of *Bits and Pieces* and has designed projects for numerous other books.

Christa Watson

An award-winning sit-down machine quilter, Christa designs quilt patterns, teaches workshops, and is the author of two machine-quilting books, both available from Martingale. Christa enjoys being a wife to her husband and a mom to her three kids. You can find her at ChristaQuilts.com.